The Words In The Wind

Zoe Shkolnik

BookLeaf Publishing

India | USA | UK

Presentation by *BookLeaf Publishing*

Web: www.bookleafpub.com

E-mail: info@bookleafpub.com

ISBN: 9789360941598

First edition 2024

To eleven year old me,

I couldn't have done it without you.

PREFACE

"The Words In The Wind" is my back and forth tug of war with accepting my own mind in the best way I know how to elucidate it. It explores my odyssey from coming to cognizance with my madness to making peace with it. This process did not happen in the span of 21 poems, it took entire lifetimes to become the girl behind this book.

Before writing "The Words In The Wind" I'd been feeling like the best thing I could do with my hands is write. Through the process of writing this book I've found that my hands still exist when I'm not holding a pen. I've realized that there is so much more I can do with these palms that means just as much. Embracing a loved one, a friendly high five, holding open a book with just my thumbs. I take my hands and place them firmly into the dirt, I am absorbing the light and life of billions of lives right through my fingertips. This love bubbles inside my chest and flushes my cheeks a bright red. In "The Words In The Wind" I hope you find solace in your own craziness, through this book I send my love to you. Treat it well, tuck it into bed at night the same way I tuck my dreams in the space between these stanzas, coddle it the same way I did these words. I get down on bruised knees and pray that you find your peace in the sun's warmth and within these pages.

Crazed Humanity

I've fallen into love with my own madness.
My lunacy is the water that falls from the
shower head and crashes on the sand,
It is the mountains and the carved out canyons,
the sky and space.
My instability is my whole world, one I can't
imagine leaving.
Nobody walks this earth holding the hands that
created it like I do.

I swallow pills like candy and say goodbye to
my crazed humanity,
Where I grew forehead lines and my hair turned
silver.
You can tell from the dents in my car and from
the cracks in my lips,
I miss it like my childhood home.
I still haven't found where to put these lonely
hands.

Standing at the foot of insanity like an ant
looking up at a mountain,
I can't help but be filled with an alluring desire.
An esoteric view I share with only a few,
I wrap my arms around it.

Shielding my greatest sin from your shallow
gaze.

I know the feeling of falling through the clouds
into the darkest depths of the abyss,
Better than I know what I am truly longing for.
I've found what i'll live for and i'm placing it
into the palms of a boxer,
Betting on him to clench his fists.
What else am I to do with this love that drips
from my nose like a bleed?

Return my love to me, my feet are cold and my
arms have fallen asleep.
I've never felt a love like this, a love so evil, a
love so pure, it takes the breath from my lungs
without warning and tells me to sing.
I lost grip of sanity and let go of the cold winter
nights that had been tangled between my toes,
I lost my mind and gained a life long
relationship.

Trepidation

I cannot feel love without trepidation.
As if all my feelings are diseased,
I feel emotions in my veins and hear my
heartbeat in my ears.

I cannot live without fearing my consciousness
has been warped once more.
Scared my head has come loose,
And that I'll have to screw it back on again.

My mania is my biggest threat,
It brings earthquakes and hurricanes into my
peaceful world.
I quiver at the sight of my own instability,
Praying there is a steadying hand attached to my
big girl bike.
When I look back,
All I see is a hungry rabid animal chasing after
me.

All the women in me are tired,
Of this world's constant reinventing.
Turning everything I thought I knew to ash,
All this madness coexists inside of me.

They've split the room into thirds with painters
tape,
Each one claiming a piece of my mind.
I beg myself to become whole,
As I balance on the rim of a coin.

I Am The Sum of Everyone
I've Ever Loved

I am the sum of everyone who has ever loved
me.
My hands shake from withdrawal,
Without you in them.
Your thumbprints are imprinted on my thighs.

I miss you like I miss the sun at night.
Your love is warm and comforting,
You melt the freezer burn that has enveloped my
body.

I am a mosaic of memories from when the day
never seemed to end.
Like a haunting ghost,
I carry you wherever I go.

I am a tapestry woven out of your touch.
How can I know your body head to toe,
And not notice you in everything?

I find little fragments of you in the way I make
my coffee,
In the books I read and
In the music I dance to.

Your fingerprints are hidden in a trees bark,
I find your skin in the sunlight's bronze glow.
I find you everywhere I look, and refuse to shut
my eyes out of fear of letting you go.

Death's Door

Death's door is made from rotting cedar wood
Overtaken by vines and mushrooms that sprout
from in between the cracks,
It is deep in the forest hidden by a canopy of
leaves stemming from a thousand foot trees.

Death lives in a tiny cottage
It looks weathered and lived in,
The walls struggle to stay standing and the
ceiling threatens to come tumbling down.
Before I can even lift my hand to knock,
Death opens his door and silently waves me in.

There is a strong scent of pine needles taking up
the room
With open arms he greets me,
Offering tea with cream and sugar with water
boiled over an open fire and leaves pulled from
the flourishing garden out back.

Death hands me a handcrafted clay mug filled
with a simmering sweet drink
His eyes shift over to the well loved sofa he's
placed in the center of the room and motions for
me to take a seat.

There is no TV, or even a coffee table beside it,
Just the lone sofa with one broken leg.

I've come to Death with a question that's been
eating me alive
Death and I are old friends, going way back.
I ask him,
Why he chose not to take me on the night we
first met,
All those years ago.

I was shattered on the bathroom floor
Laying on my own broken shards,
With Death towering over me.

I ask why he chose not to step on me
Why he didn't squeeze the remaining life right
out of my ears,
Drink my soul from my nose,
And take my body for his own.

As I attempt to interrogate death
I am sitting on his sofa feeling the draft of wind
come in from the broken windows,
The sunlight lifting my dark hair with rays the
penetrate the gaps in the ceiling,
I allow it to feel me up and to ground me all at
once.

I answer a lifelong question
Death is not the thief I thought he was.
The light he claims,
Has already left the eyes.

On the night we met
All those years ago,
Death got down on his knees and tried to level
with me,
The way an adult does to a child.
From his knees he must have caught a glimpse
of life hanging on within me,
Clinging to bone, not ready to let go.

We finish our tea in a silence only broken by a
bird's song
I hand the artisan mug back to death and head
for the door,
Even with my back turned, eyes straight ahead,
Preparing for the journey through the forest back
to where Life and Love live
I catch an approving nod,
One meant to serve a job well done.

I know I won't be back here
Standing in death's doorway,
For a very long time.
It is not a tragic goodbye,
I'll meet Death again in old age.

He'll be standing over my head as I lay on white
sheets,
All pruned up with Life's kisses covering my
worn down body.

Death will look at me the same way he did on
the day we first met
All those years ago.
He will get down to his knees,
But in this future he'll lift me up gently,
And take me straight to Death's door

Longing

I know too much and still too little.
Just barely cognizant of my deep seeded
longing,
But not what for.
Your soul has been engraved on mine,
I carry you wherever I go.

The problem with nice days is,
I feel you in the brisk wind and in the sun's
warmth.
I see you in hot cups of coffee and in the people
drinking them.

I am overflowing with love for you and
I'm trying to unplug the drain.
As you lay your head on my shoulder,
You whisper "I miss you" into my hair and I
know,
That getting over you will be like holding onto
the horizon.

The people wrapped in my words become a part
of my art and
Become a part of me.

I'm spinning this bloody ache into the spiderweb
of all the things I find lovely,
My shoulders are cramped under the burden of
carrying my desire.
This longing I found between clay covered
fingers,
I'm returning it to the river it flowed through.

I've fallen in love with a new song.
I found myself dancing in the rain.
I would hug you but I am far away from where I
was yesterday.

All Fours

13

I can't seem to find where I lost my breath
I looked under the couch upstairs downstairs and
in yesterday's pant pockets

I bow down to my body
My humanity falls onto all fours

I watch myself wither away from the other side
of the lass
Though I'm not sure what side I'm on

Cold Hearted

I tried for a loveless life,
A cold hearted existence.

I saw all the love surrounding me and
Chose to close my eyes.

With nothing to lose,
What was the universe to take from me?

I was born to love,
I know love exists because I am full of it.

For years I denied this fate,
My love welcomed me with outstretched arms
and I walked the other way.

What is my love
If not a violent carnivore?

Ready to eat,
It consumes everything around me.

It goes after the trees and their leaves,
Then it chases behind my friends and finally me.

My love swallows everything whole,
It means no harm I'm sure.

But it's cold down here,
In the depths of my despairing love.

My friends wish to be free,
I can't make them stay by locking them in with
sharp teeth.

I beg for love but I beg for peace.
My love screams in my ears and punches my
chest with iron firsts.

I beg for love but I beg for light.
My love is dark and uninviting.

It is mysterious and I am a curious child,
searching every crack and crevice for the love
I'm sure has just been misplaced.

I opened my heart to a love filled life,
And you ate my heart whole in one smooth bite.

I'm still in denial,
That this love can be so cruel, even after it hurts
me time and time again.

The sun rises every morning without
condolence,
Shining on the broken pieces that have become
of my body.
I wish to melt into the dirt,
To return to the last place I called home.

For better or for worse,
I will go back to my loveless life.

I'm taking my nails and scraping my insides
clean,
Trying to get rid of all this love I house inside of
me.

Nobody deserves to be loved by me,
I will keep this rabid animal I call my love.

Locked away,
Deep inside of me.

My Art

I'm milking my despair for art
Pressuring my words into spilling from my eyes
and into a glass cup
I'll use my misery to wet my paintbrush
I'll turn this melancholy into something that
makes my suffering worth enduring at last

I upbraid my sentences, scold my stanzas
For not following the choreography
We've been practicing this dance for years
This performance is meant to awe,
What was it all for if I failed to draw a crowd?

My feet are enervated and bruised,
At least a ballerina has something to show for
bleeding toes
I've been to rock bottom and came up for air
with empty hands
Madness creeps in through my ears and takes the
reins on my brain
I wish I could put down the pencil but I've been
sentenced to a life of everlasting inadequacy

I demand my words stand up and run through
the routine again,

No matter how many times I dive into
disconsolation and fail to find any signs of
reason,
I'm still holding onto hope for dear life

There has to be something that manifested from
my survival
Something that validates my every breath
Something that shows I have not taken all these
punches for nothing
Bruised and beaten,
What was it all for?

Lament

When did this loneliness turn hard?
When did it become a ragged stone cursing my
calloused feet?

I miss the comfort I found it dewy spring
mornings and snow kisses winter nights

When did my love go cold?
My boiling hot heart has been reduced to a boil
then rendered still.

I miss being able to soak up the world in it's
veracity,
To feel it's love enter me through my fingertips

The dirt has a heartbeat,
You can see it pulsate in the swaying grass
You can feel it in the brisk wind

When did my longing dull?
My ambitions were razor sharp,
Now I fail to pierce even my own skin with my
thirst.

I miss my oblivion and my bliss,

I wish to feel the light of a thousand suns on my
face,
I mistook thunder for tenderness and
earthquakes for intimacy
I wish I never felt the ground tremble and shake

A Lorn Less Love

I am earth
Dancing upon earth

My feet leave imprints on the dirt and
With every step
I soak up the impossibility of it all

The absurdity that runs through my veins
Is everything but emollient

I only wish to sleep
Without dreams of sucking the eternal
knowledge out of the stars
With a straw

I fear that the more cognizant I become
The more I wither away

I observe the world in parts
Taking it in its entirety one at a time
Trying to fall in love with the lunacy of every
little thing

To understand how crazy it is
To be breathing atop a breathing planet

A ballet dance spinning with grace,
How lucky am It to be watching such an awing
performance
From a front row seat

The Battle

I spend nights awake mourning who I could
have been,
Had I not thrown myself way,
Left myself for dead.

I come crawling back to myself every time,
Blistered and bleeding with a heart full of
resentment.

I dare to fight fire with fire,
Kill myself as I tried to kill me.
My brain and body are charging at each other
with pitchforks in hand.

My entire life has been war,
A never ending fight between me and what isn't
there.
A standstill fight on no man's land just to feel
the air.

I'm standing on one side of a room pointing a
gun,
I'm sitting on the other side of the room shaking
in fear.

My heartbeat is a warning siren,
My feet drop like bombs with every step,
My bones crack like fire,
Where can I hide from this violence when it
stems from me?

You cannot kill me,
My own invincibility enrages me,
My helplessness as I fail to rip my life from my
own hands.

Death's cold hands wrap around my face,
His breath slides across my cheek.
Marking his territory, I am no longer mine.
Was I ever?

The Writers Oydssey

25

I don't have faith in my words,
I believe the paper has been tainted by my
endless prattling,
It screams in my ear and begs to be ripped out,
no longer pure.
I'm trying to paint a picture worth a thousand
words with three,
And failing miserably.

My hands were molded with a clay straight from
the cold stream that runs through my veins,
I was made to hold a pen to paper.
This is my greatest tragedy,
We are star crossed lovers,
My words and I.

I wish on shooting stars for someone to hold me
the way I coddle these letters.
For someone to tuck me into bed at night the
way I tuck my dreams in the space between my
stanzas.

This lovelorn makes my stomach turn.
I was the last in my class to learn to read and
write,

As if the universe never wanted to unlock this
Pandora's Box that lies within the darkest depths
of my throat.

My head is filled with sprinting sentences.
Nauseated by the circles they scamper,
I vomit words as if I had Spaghettio's for lunch.
They're trying to escape me as if my tongue is a
prison cell,
Sentenced to an eternity of inadequacy.

I rip apart canvases and notebooks with my bare
teeth,
I expect my poems to reach the stars,
I need to hold them in my palms, and steal
everything they withhold.
Like the secret to good art is being dangled right
in front of me,
I'm no better than a dog chasing a ball into a
busy street.

I attempt to snuff myself out like a fire,
I shut my mouth with a padlock and tie my
fingers together with twine,
Attempting to drown my own mind.
A mountain i've climbed too many times,
Standing atop of Everest, alive and irritated.

The words gush out of my nose like a bleed,

I'm afraid all this violence might never be
enough for me.
I'm afraid I'm trying to be something I was
never meant to be.
I brush parise off my shoulders and eat criticism
like air.

I want nothing more than to contribute to the
museums,
To the shelves in my favorite bookstores.
I find it so incredibly difficult to observe a
mosaic and not feel helpless in the presence of
something so beautiful,
Knowing nothing I ever create will be as soft
and tender as this,
I want my writing to fall off the paper like meat
from the bone.

I'im trying to be more gentle,
Instead of upbraiding my stanzas for tripping,
I'm kissing their scraped knees.
If my poetry is a seedling begging for water and
warmth,
Water and warmth is what I shall give.
My writing has a long way to go,
These words are not fully grown. '

I'll cradle them in my arms until they mature.
I'm holding onto the back of their first two wheel
bike,
Steadying them until they're ready to go alone.
I have faith that they'll fly into the right ears and
find home in other hearts.

Seventeen

I celebrate longevity,
I dance with my forehead wrinkles and smile
lines.

I have the privilege of waking up everyday to
greet the sun's familiar face,
I get to listen to new music, read new books, and
learn new words.

I get to feel sadness and happiness and every
emotion in between,
I get to accept them and feel them in their
veracity.

I get to hold love in my heart and in the palms of
my hands,
And absorb its warmth.

Because the world did not end when I was nine,
Or ten, or eleven, or twelve.

I want to grow old,
I want to learn how to knit and how to fly.

Let me celebrate a wisdom,

That comes from the blessing of well being and
crows feet.

Because the world did not end when I was
thirteen,
Or fourteen, or fifteen, or sixteen.

I turn seventeen in June.
And I still believe my world ended every year in
between.

Worlds end all the time,
But that doesn't mean they stop spinning.

They have to end, to make room for a new one,
Like a shirt to grow into.

My nine year old world could not have held,
All this love.

I do not resent everything I gained for
everything I lost
Not anymore.

Can You Come Over?

Can you come over?
I have enchiladas in the oven and horchata in the
fridge,
Let's lay in front of the fireplace under a soft
blanket with hot mugs of tea while snow falls
outside, I want to be there when you witness
winter for the first time.
We can drive up the Rocky Mountains, I can
show you the best views,
Standing above the clouds, I can read you all the
poems I wrote to you,
Or we can breathe the fresh Mile High City air
in silence, it doesn't matter.
All that matters is your breath in my hair.

I look up at the stars and bow down to my knees,
Wishing away the state lines that separate our
night skies.
This is the first love i've known not to be lorn,
No matter where you are, I make you a plate at
dinner every night,
There will always be an open chair in my heart
waiting for you,
Hurry over before this meal grows cold.

Can you come over?
I'd walk to California if there was no other way,
Eight hundred and three miles is nothing in the
face of my longing.
You send me postcards and letters, I have pages
full of you,
And it is still not enough.
I need to hold you in the pupils of my eyes for
more than a passing glance.
I need to introduce you to my parents and my
friends,
I know you'd get along.

Let me walk you through the halls of my life
outside of my phone screen.
I need to hear your voice from across the dinner
table,
The daily phone calls fail to satisfy my desire.
I carry a picture of you everywhere I go,
So I never have to feel alone.

Can you come over?
Can we make pillow forts and stay up late
watching nostalgic movies?
We can eat candy for breakfast and wear
mismatched socks.
I want to relive my childhood with you,
Not the one we got but the one we deserved.
I think my entire life i've been waiting for you,

For a love as soft and tender as this one.

The universe sang to me and you were it's song,
I'll follow your melody to the ends of the earth.
From the day that we first met, it has been you.
It has always been you.
The world went quiet the second I laid eyes on
you.
It's you, and it always will be.
I always thought love hit and scratched and
bruised,
This love is serenity, it is peace.

Can you come over?
I'm tired of writing to you alone.
I dedicate my thoughts to you,
I am just as much mine as I am yours.
In every lifetime I know we are together,
I could live a million lives and never forget
about you.
I promise to send you a postcard from every
universe I find myself in.
I'd deliver them to you myself if there was no
other way.

I promise one day, we'll walk on the same dirt.

I won't have to get on a plane to see you, I'll be
able to walk out of my room and find you sitting
on the living room couch, reading a book.
I want to watch the leaves change from green to
purple with you,
Let's watch the grass grow tall and the flowers
bloom.
You are the sun to my moon,
The love to my life.

Insanity's Ballad

I found myself crying with my head between my
knees at the end of an infinite hallway when the
doors suddenly unlocked themselves and flew
open violently.
I run to the moon and farther, barely looking into
each room.
None of them hold what I desire,
The contents of my most sentient dreams.
I am exactly who I see in my visions,
My life, one very detailed fantasy.

The night shift workers are lowering their blinds
in frustration, the morning shift workers are
pressing snooze just once more.
The excitement is rising in my chest and spilling
out of my nose like a bad cold.
Mania is helium in my lungs,
My own insanity undoes the stitches holding me
together and undresses me,
It ties me to a steak and salivates over my body
on the menu tonight.

Insanity tears apart the threads connecting the
sky and the land,
Blurring the line between fact and fiction.

I cannot trust anything I think is real,
I'm worried that If I reach out to hold onto my
future, my hands might fall right through.

Sanity forgive me,
I'm letting the madness consume me just once
more.
How else will I find out the heights I can reach?
I dare the stars to outlast me and laugh at their
losses,
Knowing I challenged them to an impossible
game.
The world becomes a bright neon, I dance on air.

Lost without my cognizance,
Unaware that i'm falling through the clouds,
Hurdling towards the ground head first.
Despair bares it's yellow teeth when it smiles at
me,
I lose my head time and time again

Pages Full of You

37

Every thought I have is dedicated to you
In my head, there are letters ill never send with
your name on them
Words with your home address run circles in my
stomach,
Eager to be set free
I vomit my love onto postcards and college ruled
paper

Every place I go, you're in my pocket like a
hand to hold
You're in every poem I write,
You're in every sentence that drips from my
mouth sweet like syrup
You are the space between my stanzas,
My love is tucked in between these letters

I have pages full of you,
And i'm afraid I still yearn for more
My arms grasp at air where your body should be

This is a confession from the other side of your
closed door
Ive never love a soul in this way
It's bruised and bloody and beautiful

An esoteric hue, created just for you
This poem comes straight from the morning
birds
They're telling the story of a girl who's found
home in your calloused hands

Dead Girl Walking

Crows circle my head
Waiting for me to fall asleep at night
So they can take me as their own
They can smell my rotting bones and the mold
harboring in my humanity from the sky
My insanity amounts to nothing but one big
meal

My body shakes like a blade of grass on a soccer
field
Terrified of being trampled
The sun rises in the morning and shines through
my windows without condolence
I take in breath and let it go in threes
I'm counting the fingers on my hands
Just to make sure I'm still me
That I'm here and not back in that house
Where the walls taught me how to tremble
The beds taught me how to run and hide
The windows taught me the hushed whisper that
has become my voice

My hair is falling out in clumps and I have
cavities between my teeth
I'm fighting off the devil with my bare hands,

My soul defies the limits of life and plays with
death like they are old friends
She dances on air and soars into the clouds,
leaving me here on the ground all alone
I belong in the dirt with last seasons leaves

Where Have I Misplaced My Head This Time?

I am the master of moderation, the ruler of
routine.
I gave up my autonomy for hands that help me
cross the street.

This is me giving up.
This is me giving in.

I'm washing down my grief with decaf coffee,
Trying to grab the reins of this indomitable
illness with all my strength.

With a strict bedtime,
I keep the tide low.

Is there anything I can do to atone for letting
myself go to waste?
I'm smoking a pack a day and looking for purity
at the bottom of each box.

I'm digging my fingernails into the dirt to find
hope,
So far all i've found is home

The Calm Before The Storm

Can we sit on top Colorado's tallest mountain,
just us in the chilly November air?

Let's snuggle up under a blanket and I'll pour
tea from a thermos as you point out the
constellations you can only see from out here.

Accompanied by nothing but each other and the
singing wind as it warns the ground of incoming
snow,

Can I write you a poem before it gets here?

There is not much I hold in these hands, I clutch
onto my love but it runs away,

Like a stream, passing through my tangled
fingers with ease.

And still, you sit with me in the freezing cold on
a rigid mountain and nod your head while I tell
you about everything below us.

I wish I could bottle this calm and seal the lid
with wax.

Take it everywhere I go.

Survival

43

My entire life, I've been teaching my body how
to die.
Preparing it for what I thought was inevitable,
For when my hands go cold and my heart runs
dry.

Lately I've been pressing my nails into the dirt
and scraping at the ground,
Trying to slow the earth's turn as I retrace my
steps
I'm out in the heavy snow looking for myself,
Looking for all the time that's gone to waste

I've been searching for where everyone buys the
light behind their eyes.
I imagine they find it in Peruvian skies and
French coffee,
God knows I've been longing for a different set
of stones to curse on my morning walks.

I don't want this coming to be and then not to be,
I want there to be a story to tell my children
while they're all tucked into bed at night.

My entire life, I've been swatting away the hands
offered to me.
I balance on the high beam with calloused feet
and keep from swaying in the wind.
I've been prying the fingers off my wrists and
rejecting all the love that floats my way,
Believing my body is not here to stay.

I'm coming to accept these hands,
I'm allowing them to raise my mind out of the
depths of this profound lunacy.

The empty pill bottles laying on my carpeted
floor,
I can't seem to throw my trophies away.

As if sickness is just a battle waiting to be won,
Have I won?

In total veracity,
I'm terrified that if I open my hand to take
yours,
All the words I've been storing in my palms will
fall back down into the pit I rose from.

Who am I without my manic creativity?
Without my depressive imagination?
I'm afraid that these cuts and scrapes will heal as
long as i'm breathing,

That this pain means nothing if I survive it.

If I open my heart up to life and love,
Where will my desperation live?
I swore myself to a life of infinite fidelity to my
own misery,
I cannot leave it out on the cold streets all alone,
As much as I wish to sit in front of the fireplace
in peace.

My entire life, I've been coming to terms with
my own instability.
Tell me brightness stems from this everlasting
night,
That if I return to the past, it will be there
waiting for me.

Desire

I'm swimming in a sea of my own helplessness.
Would you still love me even if I was no use to
you?

Is there a love that transcends hunger?
I want to both hate and hold you closer.

I'm borrowing grief from the future,
Feeling the despair of events that have yet to
mature.

You are there air that went away,
I grasp at something that isn't there.